京华龍影

Beijing's Dragons

朱天纯　摄影　撰文

Photos and Text by Zhu Tianchun

学苑出版社

Academy Press

目录

序言

　　龙，对于中国人，是比较熟悉的一个形象。中国人已经习惯把自己称为龙的传人。而外国人了解中国的龙，除了神话传说、科幻小说的艺术想象之外，很大程度是受中国文化的影响，接受和认识龙这个本身就是一种传说的艺术形象。

　　龙的起源，虽然也有一些虚拟想象的神话动物与龙相近，可要确切的寻找出龙产生年代的有力论据，绝非易事。中国的史前文化是多元的，出现在各类型文化中的原龙纹也是多元的，因此龙的起源也应当是多元的。这些起源于多元的原龙纹在经过了长时间的共存之后，最终融合为一体，相对稳定地延续到商文化中。如果我们把文字的出现和使用作为一种印证的话，龙字始见于中国目前所知最古老的文字商代甲骨文和金文中。据专家统计，商代甲骨文中的龙字多达七十多种，这样我们至少可以推论，龙的概念是形成于商代之前。由于中国文字的象形性，从这些甲古文的形象上归纳，大概分成了两类，虽然存在着较大差异，但它们都明显呈现出动物的形态。

　　最早论及龙的生态特征的文字当属《周易》，而孔子对于龙的论述就更多了，至于后来战国时期的韩非子、汉代的刘向，都有关于龙的清晰论述。汉代许慎《说文》把龙说成一种多变的神性动物："鳞虫之长，能幽能明，能细能巨，能短能长，春分而登天，秋分而入渊。"这一说法几乎成了龙的定义。而我们目前所见最早描述龙的具体形象的记载，似乎是明代李时珍《本草纲目》中所引的后汉学者王符的言论："（龙）其形有九似，头似驼，角似鹿，眼似兔，耳似牛，项似蛇，腹似蜃，鳞似鲤，爪似鹰，掌似虎，是也。其背有八十一鳞，具九九阳数。其声如戛铜盘，口旁有须髯，颔下有明珠，喉下有逆鳞。"龙的这种九似的奇异

1

形象一直延续到明清，到现在也没有多大的变化。

　　龙文化在史前有着众多的渊源聚合，而龙文化的形成，在商代终于水到渠成。由于商王朝的建立，使得龙文化的形成具有了物质基础。龙这样一个艺术形象的出现，是人类早期艺术创造者们的宗教心理和艺术观念的综合产物。当物质基础与意识需求两者齐备时，龙文化作为一种新生事物的出现也是必然的。于是乎，各种经过化合式变形而形成的龙的形象，终于在各种实体器物上精彩地展现了。

　　龙是中华民族进入农业社会后创造的一种虚拟艺术形象，是我国古代传说中的灵异神物，亦万兽之首。而龙本身所寄托的人们的种种臆想，也是龙文化的重要组成来源。上古时期的龙，是人神通天的助手和坐骑，是影响云雨河泽的神兽，也是寓意吉祥的瑞兽，在民间龙王庙几乎是随处可见，龙王爷也是老百姓最熟悉的神仙之一。中国又是传统的农业大国，靠天吃饭是老百姓的头等大事，所以人们祈福迎祥祝愿灾年九龙治水，求龙王带来风调雨顺的好日子。这是龙文化中因宗教需要而产生的属性。而龙与政治的关系，则是龙文化之所以形成发展的重要原因。当我们回顾龙诞生过程的时候，就会发现，龙是由商朝的统治者对"远方图物"进行综合融解而创造出来的产物。在产生之初，必然会不可避免地带有强烈的政治垄断色彩。虽然随着各个朝代的瓦解更替，龙文化一度走向了百姓的生活，然而进入了封建社会之后，统治者为了统治权威，想要使龙成为他们的专属工具，龙（形象）的使用，从民间开放，走向了封建垄断。这个创造、发展、再到垄断的变化，从一个侧面也反映了中国政治制度的发展演化过程。

　　历史上的各个朝代对于龙的垄断都有着明确的法典规制。例如在东汉，皇家就对龙纹的使用做了明文限制，九卿以下的官员在祀典中已无使用龙纹的资格；元世祖忽必烈明文规定市街商店不得织造或贩卖日月龙凤纹样的缎匹；而明王朝开国皇帝朱元璋出身贫寒，需要借助龙神化自己，加强威信，从而制定了一套以不同动物纹饰表示官职地位的规定，而龙纹只是皇家专属。这说明了封建王朝的统治者垄断龙（文化）专属自己，无非是想借助通天的神兽来映射自己非同凡人，以维持其统治地位而已，所以到了封建社会的末期，龙也就成了封建帝王的标志性纹样。既然封建时代龙是帝王的象征，也就用来指帝王和帝王相关的东西：龙种、龙颜、龙廷、龙袍、龙宫等，龙文化也就达到了与封建统治阶级政治需要密切联系的鼎盛时期。

　　客观讲，龙虽然可以作为中国文化非常典型的一种民族文化艺术形象，但还是不能把它完全等同为中华民族的图腾标志。图腾据《现代汉语词典》的解释："原始社会的人认为跟本氏族有血缘关系的某种动物或自然物，一般用作本氏族的标志。"至少四个要素是龙所不具备的：原始社会、本氏族、血缘关系、动物或自然物。

　　虽然龙不是严格意义上的中华民族图腾，但是龙的身上确实具备了很多图腾文化所具备的特性，延伸到我们所能见到的各种龙的形象，使我们深深体味到龙的各种内涵外延变化，体会到各种吉祥的寓意，也能深深地感悟到中华民族文化修养的底蕴和精神。

　　上下数千年，龙已渗透了中国社会的文化，除了在中华大地上传播承继外，还被远渡海外的华人带到了世界各地，最多和最引人注目的饰物仍然是龙。因此，"龙的传人"也获得了世界的认同。

一、了解龙文化的博大精深

龙生九种，种种不一。龙生九子，本来是一种民间传说的泛指，有着不同的版本，这和中华民族地域广阔、民族文化丰富有关。约定俗成虽然是九子，但仅笔者搜集的一些资料，还是不尽相同，而且更有一些"侄、甥"，虽然可能不是"直系"龙子，但在中华民族的文化传承之中，也把它们视为"龙子"。了解了这些知识，我们就可以从北京皇家宫殿、园林建筑；历代文物、极品珍藏；民间文物、工艺作品这几个方面，寻找龙痕鳞影。

二、北京地区是中华龙文化的首善之区

我所拍摄的龙照片，基本上是在北京拍摄的。在北京，可以相对集中地有深度地挖掘这个悠久深远的题材。北京是七朝古都，"龙"这一集皇权思想之最的"图腾"形象，京城是最集中、最完整、最丰富、最典型的展现之地。集中北京一地虽然是一个限制的因素，但也给自己一个条理化探讨这个课题的框架，可以相对集中地从某一典型地域的题材来谈论这个广泛宽阔的话题。

在华夏土地上有过曾经作为诸侯国都的其他旧朝古都，从封建礼法上说，龙是不可能、也绝不允许出现在其他这些地方的。虽然个别地方也有一些龙的形象出现，除了历史皇家遗迹因素所在，至少这些地方不是"敕赐"就是"敕封"。所以真正京城之外龙形象出现的地方，很多都是有皇封谕旨之后，才能在规制之内建塑龙的形象，所以我们可以有根据地说，龙这一形象，在北京首屈一指，无可争议。如果能够把北京的龙形象，基本上形成一定数量资料积累的话，肯定会对全国以至全世界龙课题的研究，起到关键性的作用。因此，我在北京尽最大能力把接触到的各个领域、年代、层次与龙有关的资料搜集上来，把这些资料分类归科，通过这些资料的整理，为中华民族龙文化的理解认识提供更加清晰的论据。

举世闻名的九龙壁，产生于明代建筑中使用龙纹的鼎盛时期。北京有两块九龙壁，一块在故宫皇极殿门前，一块在北海北岸天王殿西。难能可贵的是，北京北海九龙壁是双面的。上面腾飞的龙具有高度的艺术水平，经专家学者鉴定，在我国龙的演变中是形象最为完美的。而故宫的九龙壁也有一个小故事：其中一条龙的烧制好的琉璃构件，在构建前摔毁了，这可是杀头之罪。聪明的工匠们，用木质材料雕刻出一块可以乱真的构件，包浆粉刷天衣无缝，骗过了当时的验收，躲过了一场弥天大祸。经过岁月的洗礼，这块木料补件也露出了本来的面目。有兴趣的朋友，可以到故宫九龙壁去一睹真相。

在故宫内的御路丹陛石，太和殿、中和殿和保和殿的台基相连成"土"字形，是取象鼎卦，取正统之意。保和殿后阶陛中间有一块雕刻着云、龙、海水和山崖的丹陛石，人们称之为云龙石雕。这是紫禁城中最大的一块石雕，长16.75米，宽3.07米，厚1.70米，重为250吨。据说是原明代雕刻，清代乾隆时期又重新雕刻。这块丹陛石石料产自京西房山大石窝。据说，当时拖运这样重的巨石用了数万名民工，修路填坑，在运送石料的道路两旁。每隔一里左右掘一口井，在隆冬严寒滴水成冰的日子，从井里汲水泼成冰道。两万民工一千多

头骡子，用了整整 28 天的时间，才运到京城。那么这块丹陛石真是这样运来的吗？乍一听很有道理，但稍加分析便会发觉漏洞百出。泼水冻冰要冻多厚才能让这重达百吨的石料经过？骡子属于硬蹄动物，在光滑的冰面上如何行走？据清史学家、清朝陵寝研究专家徐广源先生查阅清宫档案得知，这石料是用练车拉来的。所谓练车就是一种低矮的平板车，最多的有 16 个轮子，因为载重量大，所以这些轮子都是木制带铁瓦的，运送大重量石料常常选在冬季，土地冰冻结实的时候。

我们看到故宫内三大殿的丹陛石石雕，分为上、中、下三层，图案对称，错落有致，浑然一体。石雕边框均采取浅浮雕的练花缠枝纹，下端为江水奔腾、尖峰耸立的海水江崖纹，突起的祥云层层缭绕，衬托着蟠龙飞升之势。当我们面对这样的龙文化的精品之作，不仅能感受到石雕主题扑面而来的那种江山代代下传、真龙天子驾驭其上的封建文化理念，而且感受到创作制造这精美绝伦龙纹御路的民工们的艺术想象力，这些普通老百姓按照自己的生活经历设想龙的意境。

北京作为中国的首都，有着得天独厚的文化资源，如果我们能够认真踏实地去公园、博物馆参观学习，收获绝对是难以计算的。我个人产生拍摄龙题材的动机，就是起源于北京大钟寺博物馆。

北京大钟寺博物馆，始建于清雍正十一年（1733）年正月，告成于雍正十二年冬。大钟寺原名觉生寺，因寺内保存有一口"大明永乐年吉日制"的大铜钟——华严钟（现称永乐大钟）而举世闻名。博物馆收藏有不同时期的各类古钟藏品，是我国唯一以古钟为专题的博物馆。当我走进博物馆的展室时，用"惊呆"这个词一点也不为过。除了这些古钟本身承载的历史知识之外，这么大的古钟竟然铸有这么精美绝伦的图案。而当我端详钟钮（也就是龙生九子的蒲牢）时，栩栩如生的龙，活灵活现地与你进行着灵魂上的交流，让你久久不愿离去。什么叫折服，什么叫倾倒，一切赞美的话语，在这些艺术珍品面前，都是多余的。我当时就下决心，一定要把北京能够见到的龙，用手中的相机拍摄下来，为北京的龙文化传播做一点实事。

三、拍摄龙题材的一些心得体会

如何拍摄北京的龙题材，自己有一些感受。

首先，要学习掌握相关的知识，有的放矢地拍摄。

相关知识主要是三个部分：一部分是上面提到的关于龙文化本身的知识。第二部分是要有明确的目标，要知道目标地处哪个地区方位。这方面的资料，既要注意在文字记载的图书画册中搜集记录，也要利用现代化的网络搜集相关信息。关键一点，在日常的外出拍摄或旅游活动的时候，要时刻注意景点周边的散落景物，或许这些不见经传的文物，就是龙文化的真传极品。还有一部分知识，就是龙造型的载体材质。龙的造型主要体现在建筑上，其次是文物，再就是彩绘，还有就是器皿。譬如建筑上龙的造型会出现在什么部位，采取什么材质，运用什么形式。再比如彩绘，一般分为和玺彩绘、旋子彩绘、苏式彩绘，而龙造型主要采用和玺彩绘，旋子彩绘也有，而苏式彩绘基本就很少见了，如果了解了这些相关的知识，对于我们找寻龙的造型会有很大的帮助。

其次，拍摄龙文化这一课题，有两方面的审美衡量尺度。一方面是搜寻龙文化的各种资料，正确客观地记录现存的历史文物的确切风貌和现代工艺珍品的艺术魅力，从而为龙文化的探根求源，提供坚实可靠的信息；另一方面是艺术地表现龙文化的千姿百态，使各种造型的龙、各种材质的龙、各种环境中的龙，通过拍摄者的镜头，充分运用摄影语汇，尽善尽美地把龙这一中华民族的典型符号，推向世界文化之林。

还有，我们是用摄影的形式来表现龙文化的魅力神姿，那么，就要充分调动摄影语汇来刻画表现客观存在的每一个龙造型。无论是记录资料或艺术表现，除了对焦精确、曝光准确、构图悦目、后期完善之外，有几点是拍龙题材时自己的一些经验：

1．虽然我们拍摄的对象是没有生命的龙造型造物，但拍摄者一定要注意拍出"神"来，要充分利用机位、角度、色光的艺术角度，通过对于被拍摄物体的理解和寄寓的意趣，注入感情，再现龙的精神。

要想拍出神，就得用看待有生命的心理去处理画面的构思。所以，如果是艺术化表现的构思需要，则要把镜头的焦点对准龙的眼睛，这样龙的生命内涵就似乎和人的情感有了沟通。然后，根据构思的需要，设置光圈大小，控制景深，把握好主题与背景的关系，也是很关键的。

2．拍摄龙造型的各种载体，肯定涉及用光的问题，而光线来源主要分为室外自然光和室内人造光。光线的运用一方面是曝光的正确，另一方面就是科学运用色温。如果是资料搜集，就要尽可能准确地表现记录原始状态的本来色温色象，而艺术表现，就要巧妙地利用各种外界条件对于龙造型物体的色温影响，在充分表现龙造型本身风貌的前提下，利用色温的万千变化，给龙造型赋予拍摄者主观情感的无限情怀。

从我们拍摄的龙的材质分析，就应该把握这些不同材质龙的颜色，使不同材质颜色的龙，在具体环境中脱颖而出，或是情景交融风情万种。自己曾为了显示龙这种神秘莫测、扑朔迷离的神话感觉，特意设计拍摄了一组水中倒影龙的造型，很多影友见了都觉得很有意思。所以有时候，阴晴雨雪的天气，对于表现龙的题材，反而提供了一种更能展现作者艺术构思的天地。

3．龙造型除了公开展示的题材可以拍摄外，也有一部分题材，是有不同的拍摄限制条件的。这就要仔细地阅读相关规定条款，不要违规强行拍摄，但也不是一个地方全是一成不变。譬如故宫，收费的珍宝馆、钟表馆，就可以拍照，而武英殿的书画展，就不准拍摄。知道了这些细微区别，就可以区别掌握拍摄的不同方式了。还要提请注意，即使让拍照，也不能使用闪光灯，所以三脚架、快门线都是必备用品。

另外，根据我的经验，要对自己使用的相机性能有充分的了解。譬如在低照度情况下，如果不准使用闪光灯，肯定就得提高 ISO 指数。但是必须时刻注意：自己的相机在什么指数条件下就会产生噪点，什么条件下这些噪点会使拍摄的影像失去了价值意义。由于拍摄条件是随时变化的，有时候会因一时疏忽，没有转换拍摄程序，或忘记转换拍摄技术指数。我选择佳能 5DII，它有一项功能就是自动智能调整 ISO，这样就避免了拍摄对象变化时而未调整

拍摄指数的失误，尤其是在拍摄低照度不让使用闪光灯条件时。这一点经验是很实用的。

从搜集资料的经验讲，一定要在拍摄主题题材的时候，尽可能把相关的环境资料拍摄下来，如果有文字或标牌介绍，也要拍照下来。如果有更好的习惯，可以随身携带笔记本，把相关的数据记录下来，并且在后期归档时，一定要尽可能多一点地注明关键词句。

搜集资料，一方面是搜集这些硬性资料，另一方面就是搜集软性资料——与当时当地的人进行沟通。人受一句话，佛受一炷香，一定要保持亲和尊重的态度去进行沟通，也许就在这不经意的几句话中，会使你意外发现一个新的课题。当然也许会遇到沟通不理想的时候，也用不着郁闷，可以变换机位运用抢拍抓拍的形式，也能拍出别有意趣的片子。要想拍到理想的片子，接人待事的方式方法也要讲求一点艺术性的变通。

拍摄龙造型题材还有很多需要注意的问题，还需要我们在拍摄这个题材时认真思索，才能更好地拍出龙文化的博大内涵和灵性神态来。有目的、有专题地去拍摄龙文化这个题材，不仅仅是个人摄影爱好的选择，也是对于北京京味文化探求的重要组成部分。现在搜集上来的这些素材，只是北京地区龙文化的凤毛麟角，而且在艺术表现的水平上，自己也不是十分满意。但愿在众多良师益友的鼓励下，在学苑出版社的鼎力支持下，我会坚守这个题材的继续探讨，这既是对于这个课题选择方向的肯定，也是为弘扬中华民族优秀文化奉献绵薄之力的一种心意表达。

京城胡同出生，东北兵团教化，书店美工职业，摄影一生追求。
写书只为交友，图片更求师训，美善修炼童心，真情告慰人生。

朱天纯
辛卯立秋于京东云深阁

Preface

The *Long*, commonly translated as *Dragon*, is a significant cultural symbol of China. The Dragon symbol was created as a mythological creature with the advent of agricultural society. Chinese legend has it that the dragon is the leader of all animals, and has magical powers. As a cultural symbol, the dragon embodies the diverse range of imaginations over the history of China. The Dragon may not be considered a totem for Chinese culture in the strict sense, but it displays many characteristics of a totem as a typical Chinese ethnic cultural creation. Through all types of dragon images, one can feel the essence and spirit of Chinese culture.

Over the centuries and dynasties, there have been different styles of dragon. Each dynasty has its own unique "dragon culture", which reflects the tastes and powers of the time.

Beijing has been the capital city of China for seven dynasties. Dragon – the totem of each dynasty's emperor and palace decoration – represents the China's "dragon culture" development over 800 years. Beijing leads other Chinese regions in the development of folk dragon culture, in the preservation of dragon artifacts in various palaces, royal gardens and museums. Beijing's dragon collection surpasses those in other regions for its completeness, richness in style, representativeness, and sophistication. The remaining royal buildings boast a diverse range of dragon sculptures and paintings.

The author of this book has, over the years, taken tens of thousands of pictures of dragon sculptures and paintings in royal gardens and museums, as well as folk art dragon collections in various places. The author selected several hundred pictures from his vast picture collection. These rare pictures, along with thoughtful commentaries, present the Beijing Dragon to the entire country and the world, even given the inherent limitations of photography. Readers interested in China's dragon culture will hopefully be motivated to learn more.

序
言

皇家宫殿　园林建筑
Imperial Palaces and Gardens

皇家宫殿　园林建筑
Imperial Palaces and Gardens

　　北京皇家园林建筑，首先是宫殿，其次是陵寝（明十三陵）、园林、寺庙、王府，这些建筑群里都可看到"龙文化"的集中展现．北京地区的皇家建筑群也是现今留存龙造型最全面、最完整、最丰富、最典型、最精美的地方。各种样式的龙雕塑、绘画，活灵活现集萃于封建皇家建筑群之中，最典型是北海双面的九龙壁。北海的九龙壁艺术价值高，不同于其他各地的九龙壁。

　　Beijing's imperial buildings primarily consist of imperial palaces (e.g. The Forbidden City), whose grandeur, apart from the palaces in Shenyang and in Taiwan, are rarely matched in China. Besides, there are also numerous tombs (e.g. Ming Tombs), gardens, temples and mansions. In all such places dragon images are prominently displayed. These buildings integrate dragon sculptures and paintings with the architecture. To appreciate the dragon culture, Beijing's imperial buildings are the best choice, as the most comprehensive, complete, rich, typical and exquisite.

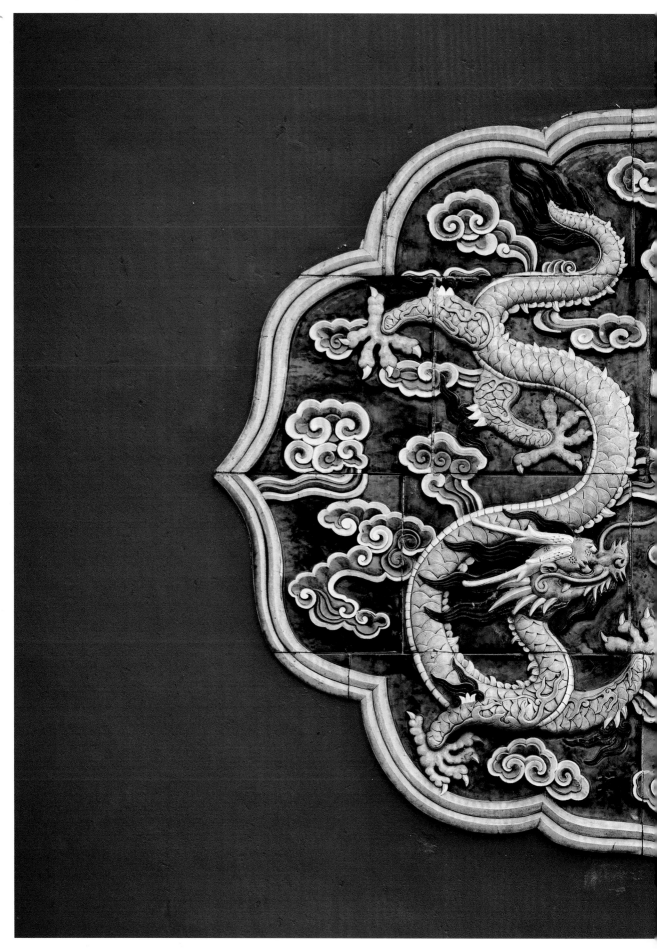

琉璃 Glazed-tile decorations

上图为北京西黄寺照壁琉璃图案，下图为故宫重华门琉璃。
Picture above is the glazed-tile screen wall of Beijing's Xihuangsi Lama Temple.
Picture below is the glazed-tile gate named Chonghuamen in the Forbidden City.

　　明清时期，琉璃建筑构件得到广泛运用，不同釉色蕴涵不同的文化象征意义。琉璃构件是中国独创的建筑材料，具有很高的建筑艺术价值和历史文化价值。

　　Glazed tiles were widely used on buildings during Ming and Qing dynasties. Different colors had different meanings. Glazed tiles are of great value for both construction and culture.

上左图为从故宫皇极门看九龙壁。
Upper left is a glimpse of the Nine Dragon Screen Wall in the Forbidden City, taken from the Gate of Imperial Supremacy.

上右图为北海西天梵境。
Upper right is the picture of Xitian Fanjing area in Beihai Park.

下图为北海琼华岛永安寺建筑群的屋脊。
Below is a picture of the roofs of Yongansi Temple on Qionghua Island in Beihai Park.

皇家宫殿　园林建筑

9

九龙壁　Nine Dragon Screen Wall

　　座落在北京北海公园北岸的九龙壁，建于乾隆二十一年（1756 年）。北海九龙壁是双面的，其艺术价值高于其他各地之九龙壁。

　　There is a Nine Dragon Screen Wall in Xiaoxitian area in Beihai Park in Beijing. It was built in 1756, the 21st year of Emperor Qianlong's reign. Since the Nine Dragon Screen Wall here is decorated on both sides, its artistic value is superior to that of its peers in other places.

皇家宫殿　园林建筑

11

一

上图为北海小西天琉璃雕塑，下图为北海九龙壁局部。
Above is the picture of the glazed-tile relief sculpture at Xiaoxitian Temple in Beihai Park,
Below is part of the Nine Dragon Screen Wall in Beihai Park.

九龙壁局部龙造型
Details from the Nine Dagon Screen Wall

鸱吻　ChiWen

　　殿堂庙宇的正中屋脊两端，有缩头卷尾张嘴吞脊的龙形装饰物，一般称为鸱吻。它被普遍认为是龙的九子之一。

　　Often seen at either end of the roof ridge of palaces and temples, this is a dragon-like decoration with crouched head, curled tail, opened mouth and hidden spine. It is a mythical animal, believed to be one of the dragon's nine children.

北京香山公园鸱吻
Chiwen decorations in Xiangshan Park in Beijing

故宫各大殿鸱吻
Chiwen decorations in the Forbidden City

　　蹲在垂脊前的一行小兽叫嘲风，其中有一个就是龙之三子，后面的龙头亦可叫作垂兽。

A row of mythical animals squatting on the roof corner are called Chaofeng, one of them is the dragon's third child. The dragon head behind is also called Chuishou.

　　明清殿堂庙宇檐角的小兽，象征吉祥，有消灾灭祸的含义。每个小兽各有其象征意义。

Small mythical animal figures are often seen on the roof corner of palaces and temples of the Ming and Qing Dynasties. They bear auspicious meanings, and are believed to able to ward off disasters.

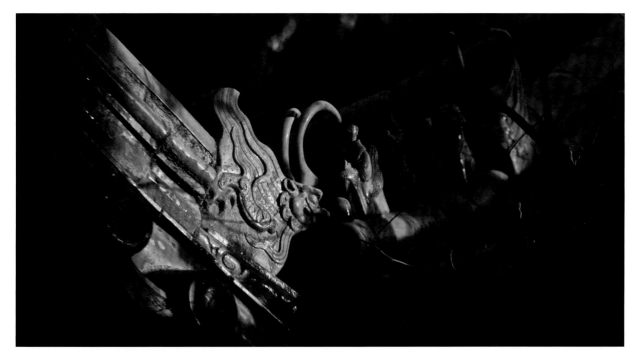

故宫及殿堂庙宇的蹲兽屋脊

Squating mythical animals on the roof corners in the Forbidden City and other buildings

下图为故宫最高等级的太和殿的屋脊蹲兽。

Below are the pictures of squating mythical animals on the roof corner of the Palace of Supreme Harmony, the highest ranking building in the Forbidden City.

瓦当　Wadang

瓦当是遮挡屋檐前端筒瓦的瓦头，古代匠人在瓦当中饰以图案。瓦当中的龙图案一般是完整的，呈现一种特殊的古拙美感。
Wadang is the round front piece of the bottom tile on the roof edge. Ancient artisans always decorate the Wadang. When the dragon image is used, it is always complete, showing an ancient beauty.

下图为北海公园西门雪后的房檐瓦当。
Below is a picture of wadang on Beihai Park's west gate after snow.

34

镇水兽
Flood Controlling Beast

左上图为地安门后门桥镇水兽。
Left is the flood controlling beast of the Houmen Bridge at Di'anmen.

右上图为通州区八里桥镇水兽。
Right is the flood controlling beast of Bali Bridge of Tongxian County in Beijing.

下图和右页图均为故宫蚣蝮。
Below and opposite are Gongfu in the Forbidden City.

蚣蝮　Gongfu

蚣蝮与龙同种，形似兽头，性好水，故多嵌刻在桥洞券面之上。

The Gongfu is similar to the dragon, good at swimming. Its image is often seen on ancient bridges.

颐和园十七孔桥蚣蝮
The Gongfu of Seventeen Arch Bridge at the Summer Palace

俯瞰故宫、太和殿蚣蝮
Looking down on the Gongfu at the Palace of
Supreme Harmony in the Forbidden

故宫御花园堆秀山蚣蝮
The Gongfu figure by the fountain of the Duixiu rockery
in the Forbidden City's Imperial Garden.

上右图为故宫御花园水池的蚣蝮。

Above is a stone carving in the pool of the Imperial Garden in the Forbidden City.

下图为故宫断虹桥桥头的蚣蝮。

Below is the Gongfu on the Duanhong Bridge in the Forbidden City.

栏板柱头　Carved Stone Banister

左页图及上图为各种不同纹样的望柱。
Above are carved banisters with different designs

下图为故宫三大殿三层汉白玉台基上面栏板柱头。
Below is the three-storey marble pedestal of one of the three grand halls in the Forbidden City.

故宫御花园钦安殿栏板
Bannister at Qin'an Hall in the Imperial
Garden at the Forbidden City

华表 Ornamental Columns

天安门前的华表
Ornamental columns in front of Tian'anmen;

北京大学图书馆门前的华表
Ornamental Column in front of Peking University's Library

五塔寺华表

十三陵御道华表

华表承露盘上有个蹲形的龙形神兽，称为犼，传说也是龙的九子之一。

There is a sculpture of a mythical animal squatting on the top of the ornamental column, It's called a Hou, one of the dragon's nine children.

御路　Imperial Way

重要殿堂殿前踏跺的中间称为御路，随着踏跺坡度倾斜铺设着的巨石雕刻。

The ramp in front of important ancient buildings is part of the Imperial Way. It was often decorated with huge stone carvings.

故宫乾清宫御路石雕

Part of the stone-carving on the Imperial Way of the Palace of Heavenly Purity in the Forbidden City

右上图为乾清宫御路石刻。

Above right is stone-carving on the Imperial Way of Qianqingmen.

右下图为故宫保和殿后三台御路云龙大石雕。

Lower right is the tri-part Imperial Way with cloud and dragon carvings behind the Hall of Preserving Harmony in the Forbidden City.

左上图为故宫乾清宫月台前蟠龙御路石雕。

Upper left is the Imperial Way with coiling dragon carvings in front of the Palace of Heavenly Purity in the Forbidden City.

下图为景山公园少年宫内的御路石雕。
Below is part of the Imperial Way in Jingshan Park.

右图为大高玄殿御路石雕。
Right is the stone-carving on the Imperial Way of Dagaoxuan Hall (an imperial Taoist temple).

故宫太极殿前石雕双龙御路
Twin-dragon Imperial Way pavement in front
of Taiji Hall in the Forbidden City.

54

故宫皇极殿御路

Detail of the stone-carving on the Imperial Way of the Hall of Imperial Supremacy in the Forbidden City

故宫内各大殿的御路石雕
Carvings from various Imperial Ways in the Forbidden City

故宫乾清宫御路石雕
Part of the stone-carving on the Imperial Way of the Palace of Heavenly Purity in the Forbidden City

故宫皇极殿御路丹石雕
Part of the stone carving on the imperial way of the Palace of Imperial Supremacy in the Forbidden City

故宫皇极殿御路石雕
Part of the stone-carving on the Imperial Way of the Hall of Heavenly Supremacy in the Forbidden City

故宫乾清宫御路石雕
Part of the stone-carving on the Imperial Way of the Hall of Imperial Purity in the Forbidden City

五塔寺石雕
Stone carvings in the Wutasi Temple

石雕
Stone Carving

上图为：北海公园琼岛春阴碑前的石雕。
Above is a stone carving on the front of the Qiongdao Chunyin tablet in Beihai Park.

中图为：故宫乐寿堂青玉云龙纹瓮。
Centre is a jade jar with cloud and dragon image from the Hall of Happiness and Longevity in the Forbidden City.

下图为：北京西四广济寺后院石雕。
Below is a stone carving in Guangjisi Temple in the Xisi area of Beijing.

京
华
龙
影

赑屃 BiXi

赑屃，也称龟趺。形似龟，平生好负重，力大无穷。长年累月驮负着石碑。人们在庙院祠堂里，经常可以见到这位任劳任怨的龙的儿子，据说触摸其头能给人带来福气。

The bixi is also called Guifu. It has a turtle like appearance. Its mighty strength makes it good at bearing weight. Always seen carrying tablets in temples and shrines, it was said to have great forbearance. Touching its head is said to bring people good luck.

左上、下图为五塔寺石碑。
Upper left and lower left are stone tablets in the Wutasi Temple.
右上图为钟楼。
Upper right is a stone tablet at the Bell Tower.
右下图为十三陵石碑。
Lower right is a stone tablet at the Ming Tombs.

门头沟白瀑寺元代石碑
Stone tablet of Yuan Dynasty at Baipusi Temple in Mentougou District of Beijing

门头沟白瀑寺辽代石碑
Stone tablet of Liao Dynasty at Baipusi Temple in Mentougou District of Beijing

狻猊 Suanni

狻猊为龙的第六个儿子，形状像狮，狮子是随着佛教传入中国的，人们顺理成章地将其装饰于香炉之上。

Suanni, the dragon's sixth child. It has a lion-like appearance. This is because the lion's image was brought to China along with Buddhism. Hence the Suanni image was often used as a decoration on incense burners.

香山八大处香炉
Incense burner at Badachu in the Xiangshan Hills

香山公园香炉
Suanni on an incense burner in Xiangshan Park

左上图为广济寺条案，右上和下图为故宫铜饰
Upper left is the Suanni on an incense burner in Guangjisi Temple;
Two other pictures are Suannis on bronze articles in the Forbidden City.

戒台寺佛坑村村头石牌坊。

The stone archway of Fokeng village near Jietaisi Temple.

砖雕 Brick Carvings

戒台寺砖雕
Brick carving in Jietaisi Temple

北京西部慈寿寺内永安万寿塔砖雕。
Brick carving on Yong'an Wanshou Pagoda of Cishousi Temple in western Beijing.

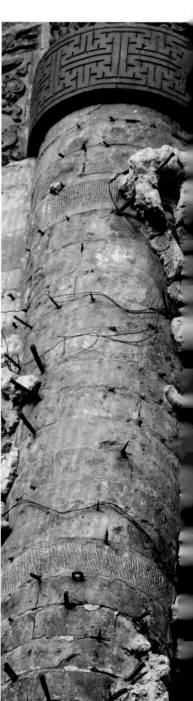

皇家宫殿　园林建筑

77

北京动物园大门砖雕。北京动物园的历史可追溯到清朝光绪三十二年（1906）。其前身是清农工商部农事试验场
Portal carving of Beijing Zoo. The zoo dates back to 1906, the 32nd year of emperor Guangxu's reign. It was once an Agricultural Experimentation Station.

左图为砖雕细部。
Left is a detail of brick carving.

碧云寺砖雕
Brick carvings in Biyunsi Temple

彩绘 Painted Decorations

　　在雄伟壮观的建筑物上施以鲜明的色彩，取得豪华富丽的装饰效果，是中国古代建筑的重要特征之一。
　　The use of bright colors on massive buildings can produce a splendid effect. It is a feature of ancient Chinese buildings.

故宫大殿内精美的彩绘
Painted decorations in the interior of grand buildings in the Forbidden City

在北京各个宫殿建筑上绘画着精美的彩绘
Exquisite painted decorations are often seen on grand buildings in Beijing

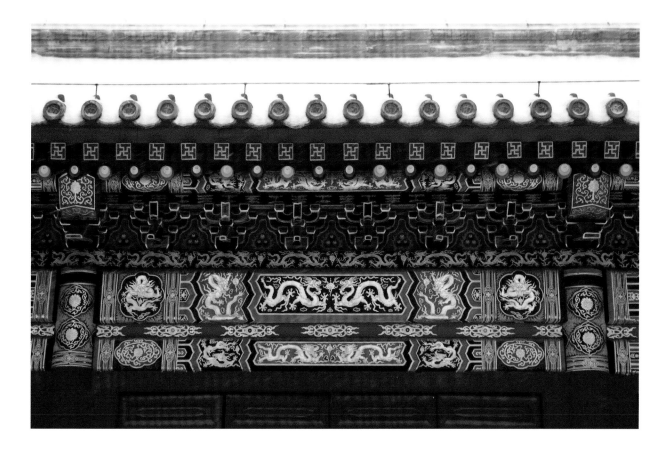

87

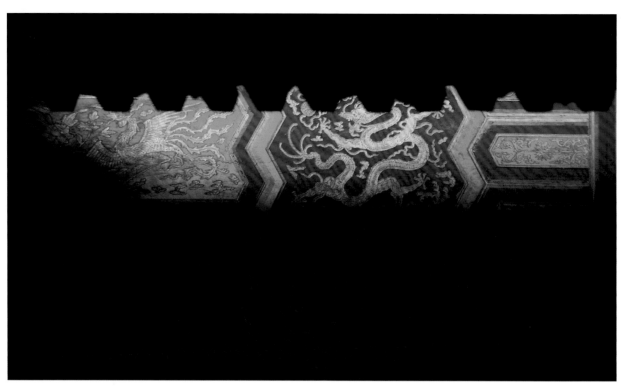

在北京各个宫殿建筑上绘画着精美的彩绘
Exquisite painted decorations are often seen on grand buildings in Beijing

木雕
Wood Carving

紫禁城各种装修工艺之精美，题材之丰富，为前代所罕见，既出于居住需要，更体现了装饰趣味及艺术水准。

The decorations in the Forbidden City show fine workmanship and rich creativity rarely seen in past dynasties. They were not only functional, but also had great artistic appeal.

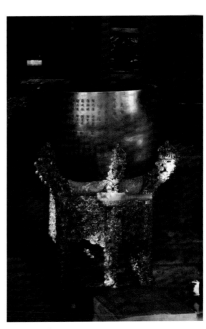

上图为故宫乾清宫内暖阁板门毗卢罩。
Above is the Pilu covering on a door in the Palace of Heavenly Purity in the Forbidden City.

下图为暖阁板门局部
Below is detail of above.

上图为戒台寺木雕佛龛，下图为故宫乾清宫内景。
Above is a carved wooden shrine in Jietaisi Temple.
Below is part of the interior of the Palace of Heavenly Purity in the Forbidden City.

故宫内门饰木雕
Carved wooden decorations on doors in the Forbidden City

乾清宮内正大光明匾
Zhengda Guangming Plaque (meaning *open and above-board*) in the Palace of Heavenly Purity in the Forbidden City.

香山公园东宫门大殿
Grand Hall at the east gate of Xiangshan Park.

太和殿慈禧题字牌匾局部
Part of the plaque with Empress Dowager Cixi's inscription in the Hall of Supreme Harmony

乾隆题字牌匾局部
Part of the plaque with Emperor Qianlong's inscription.

藻井 Zaojing

　　宫殿内的藻井，一般都用在庄严尊贵的殿宇内，藻井的结构异常复杂，非常富有装饰趣味。由于等级不同和所处环境有异，各个别具风格的藻井，都是形象美观，造型精致的艺术杰作。

　　The *zaojing* is a complicated decorative installation, often appearing on the ceiling of a grand building. Though they vary according to the rank of the building, a zaojing is always delicate and beautiful.

北京门头沟白瀑寺藻井
The Zaojing of Baipusi Temple in Mentougou District of Beijing.

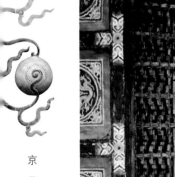

故宫御花园明代建澄瑞亭藻井
Zaojing of the Chengrui Pavilion in the Imperial Garden of the Forbidden City

故宫御花园万春亭藻井
Zaojing of the Wanchun Pavilion in the Imperial Garden of the Forbidden City.

故宫养心殿藻井
Zaojing in the Hall of Mental Cultivation
in the Forbidden City

故宫御花园明代建千秋亭藻井
The zaojing of the Qianqiu Pavilion in the
Imperial Garden of the Forbidden City

颐和园内藻井
Zaojing in the Summer Palace

故宫养性殿藻井
Zaojing in the Hall of Nature Cultivation in the Forbidden City

先农坛隆福寺藻井
Zaojing of the Longfusi Monastery in the Temple of Agriculture

故宫太和殿藻井
Zaojing in the Hall of Supreme Harmony in the Forbidden City

故宫养心殿藻井
Zaojing in the Hall of Mental Cultivation in the Forbidden City

北海小西天藻井
Zaojing of Xiaoxitian Temple in Beihai Park

上图为北京五塔寺内藻井
Above is the zaojing of Wutasi Temple in Beijing.
下图为北京大觉寺内藻井
In the lower right corner is the zaojing in Dajuesi Temple in Beijing.

京华龙影

故宫江山社稷铜亭
Jiangshan Sheji Pavilion in the Forbidden City

故宫内门窗铜饰
Bronze fittings on doors and windows in the Forbidden City

京华龙影 一

故宫御花园钦安殿獬豸
Bronze Xiezhi (a mythical animal) in front
of the Qin'an Hall in the Imperial Garden of the
Forbidden City.

故宫御花园铜香炉

A bronze incense burner in the Imperial Garden of the
Forbidden City

上下两图为北京古观象台浑天仪。

Above and below are astronomical instruments to be found in the
ancient observatory in Beijing.

上图为故宫储秀宫铜龙雕塑。
Above is a bronze dragon sculpture in front of the Palace of Gathering Excellence in the Forbidden City.

右下图为故宫养心殿前的玉璧。
Lower right is a jade disk set in front of the Hall of Mental Cultivation in the Forbidden City.

左下图为北海承露盘。
Lower left shows the decorative plate atop a column in Beihai Park.

椒图 Jiaotu

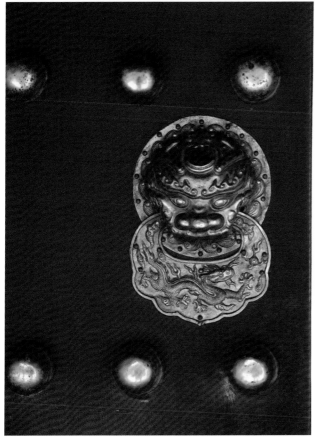

故宫内各个大门上的铜饰
Bronze decorations on doors in the Forbidden City

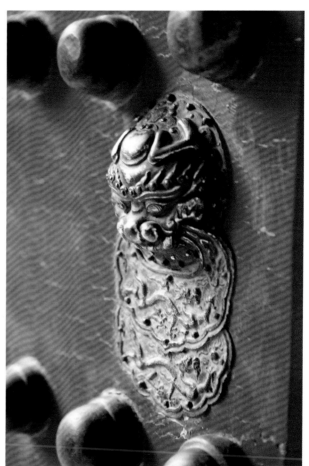

蒲牢 Pulao

　　大钟寺（觉生寺）始建于清雍正十一年正月，告成于雍正十二年冬的释门名刹，现为古钟博物馆成立于 1984 年。是收藏、研究、展览、开发、研制，利用古钟文物资源，多功能的古钟博物馆。
　　Dazhongsi Temple (i.e. Jueshengsi, or Bell Temple) was built during emperor Yongzheng's reign in the Qing dynasty. It is now a museum of ancient bells with was an immense collection of bells, a wonderful resource for research into the development of ancient Chinese bells.

乾隆铜钟
Bronze bell cast during Emperor Qianlong's Reign

永泰寺钟（康熙五十二年，1713 年）
Yongtai Bronze Bell (cast in 1713, the 52nd year of Emperor Kangxi's reign)

乾隆年间铜钟
Bronze bell cast during Emperor Qianlong's Reign

云纹铜钟（明正德八年，1513 年）
Bronze bell with cloud patterns, made in the 8th year of Zhengde,1513, in the Ming dynasty

张淮等造铜钟（明正德十五年，1520 年）
Bronze bell, made by Zhang Huai and others in the 15th year of Zhengde, 1520, in the Ming dynasty.

摩河庵铜钟（明嘉靖丙午年，1546 年）
Bronze bell from Mohean Nunnery, made in 1546, during the reign of Ming emperor Jiajing

大钟寺因殿内保存一口"大明永乐年月吉日制"的大铜钟——华严钟（现称永乐大钟）而举世闻名。
Dazhongsi (Great Bell) Temple is famous for its possession of a huge bronze bell, named Huayan Bell (now known as the Great Bell of Yongle). It was cast during emperor Yongle's reign in Ming Dynasty (ca. 1420).

永泰寺钟（康熙五十二年，1713 年）
Yongtai Bronze Bell (cast in 1713, the 52nd year of Emperor Kangxi's reign)

仁王院铜钟（1077 年）
Bronze bell from Renwangyuan

三十五佛名铜钟（明正德七年，1512 年）
Bronze bell inscribed with the names of 35 Buddhas. (Ming dynasty, 1512)

弘治道钟（明弘治壬子年，1492 年）
Hongzhi Taoist Bell (cast in 1492, under Ming Emperor
Hongzhi's reign)

铸佛铜像钟（清道光壬午午年，1822 年）
Bronze bell with cast buddha figure (cast in 1822, during Qing Emperor Daoguang's reign)

鹤纹铜钟（明代）
Bronze bell with crane figure (Ming dynasty)

饕餮 Taotie

故宫内各种大水缸随处可见，以铜质为多，原为故宫消防之具，有的大缸为铜制鎏金工艺，两耳加兽面铜环，制作精致，外表华丽，这个铜兽就是龙之一子饕餮。

Bronze water vats are frequently seen in the Forbidden City. They were for fire-fighting. The vats are exquisitely made, some are even gilded. There handles mounted on decorating rings, above which is a mythical animal called a *taotie*, one of the dragon's children.

京
华
龙
影

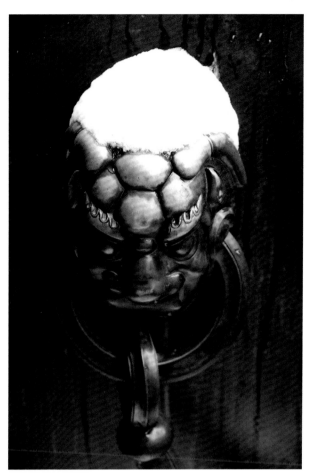

故宫雨花阁
Yuhua Pavilion in the Forbidden City

128

故宫雨花阁
Yuhua Pavilion in the Forbidden City

故宫雨花阁，是清乾隆年间仿建西藏阿里古格托林寺的一座藏传佛教密宗佛堂。
Yuhua Pavilion in the Forbidden City. It was built in imitation of a Tantric Buddhist shrine in Guge Tholing Temple in Ali area of Tibet.

　　龙，是皇家专属标志物，无论是日用的器具、饮食用具、服饰、美轮美奂的宫廷器皿还是陈设器物，都有着"龙"的造型。北京有各种各样的博物馆近 200 座，这些博物馆珍藏着很多珍贵的文物和很多北京地域"龙文化"的艺术工艺品，从这琳琅满目的文物珍品中，可以了解到各种各样的"龙文化"的历史传承和相关知识。在这里，我们从这浩如烟海的珍品之中，精选出了各个朝代的"龙"的造型。

As an exclusive symbol of the emperor, the dragon image permeated ancient court life and the vicissitudes of different dynasties, both the grand and the minute. It is a key part of all designs on garments, bedding articles, wine cups, etc.

金瓯永固杯
Gold cup inlaid with treasures

上图为明万历金蕾丝皇冠

Above is a crown of gold filigree made during emperor Wanli's reign in Ming dynasty

下图为故宫珍宝馆金嵌宝石佛塔

Below is a golden Buddhist tower located in the Forbidden City. It is decorated with gold filigree and inlaid with precious stones

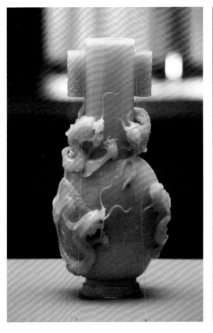

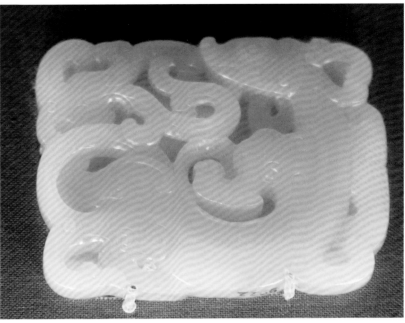

故宫珍宝馆里展览的龙的造型玉器
Dragon figured jade artefacts exhibited in the Treasure Hall of the Forbidden City

　　乾隆皇帝对前代皇帝御玺重新考证排次，将其总数定为25方，并详细规定了各自的使用范围。

Emperor Qianlong once made a thorough investigation of the imperial seals of past rulers. He set the total number at 25, and stipulated their respective significance.

故宫收藏各种皇帝专用御玺
Various imperial seals in the
Forbidden City collection

皇帝专用的御玺
Imperial seals

金嵌珍珠天球仪（乾隆年间）
Gold and pearl studded globe (Qianlong period)

带有龙的图型的蜡烛
Dragon figured candles exhibited in the Forbidden City

左图为明代皇后金蕾丝嵌宝石点翠凤冠
Left is an empress's crown from the Ming dynasty. It is embellished with golden filigree, inlaid with jadeite and diamonds.

下图为清代金龙形帽顶
Below is the top of a golden dragon crown of the Qing dynasty.

西周夔龙纹圆鼎
Round Tetrapod vat from Western Zhou
dynasty (ca 1100-771 BC) decorated with a
Kui - a kind of one legged-dragon

叠瓣龙纹鼎 春秋
Tripod with over-lapping leaves and dragon design from Spring and Autumn period (722-481 BC)

龙形帽冠架
Hat stand with dragon design

唐代双龙耳盘口壶
Flat top bottle with twin dragon handles from
Tang dynasty.

故宫展示的皇家针织刺绣珍品
Imperial embroidery exhibited in the Forbidden City.

华盖
Canopies

华盖
Canopies

绣片纹样
An embroidery piece

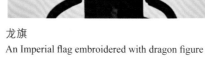

綉帐
Embroidered decoration on Imperial chariot

龙旗
An Imperial flag embroidered with dragon figure

图为清乾隆各色釉彩大瓶。
Multicolored glazed porcelain vases made during emperor Qianlong's reign in Qing dynasty.

图为青花釉里红云龙纹天球瓶（清·乾隆）

A glazed porcelain jar in blue and red, with a cloud and dragon design.
It was made during emperor Qianlong's reign in the Qing dynasty.

故宫珍宝馆展品　龙纹铜盆
Bronze basins with dragon design exhibited in the Treasure Hall of the Forbidden City

故宫展示的皇家御用马具
Imperial stirrups and saddle

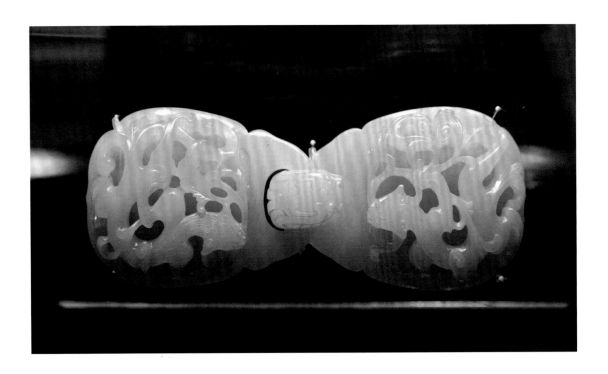

故宫珍宝馆展品 玉饰
Jade artefacts exhibited in the Treasure Hall of the Forbidden City

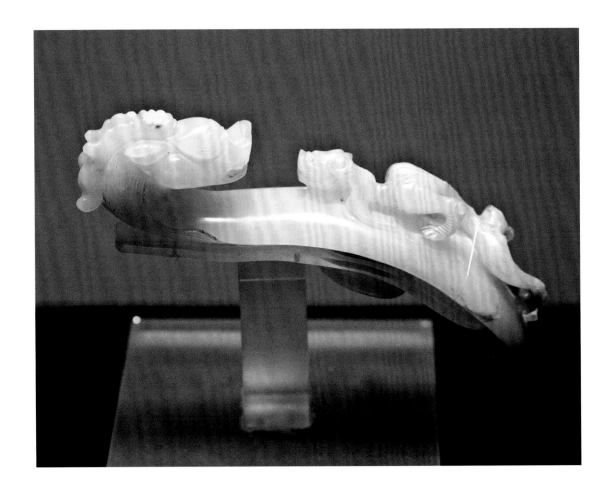

故宫珍宝馆　水晶觥

Crystal cup exhibited in the Treasure Hall of the Forbidden City

民间文物　工艺作品
Folk Collections and Artifacts

过去，北京民间也有很多建筑中有龙的造型。有些地方与皇家有着密切的关系，故其建筑、器皿、明清家具等也有各种龙的造型装饰，用龙的纹样来标明这些地方与皇家王族的不同一般的关系。

历史发展到今天，龙的形象已经完全转化为整个中华民族文化的一种艺术符号。近现代，中国的艺术家们以龙为艺术创作的典型形象，为华夏大地创作了大批超越历史局限的艺术佳作。龙的形象在广阔天地中，被赋予了更具魅力的艺术文化风韵。现代人的思维视角、工艺材料、制作技术，给龙这一形象的繁荣发展注入了新的活力，使龙这一形象有了新的传承，更具时代风范。

History has developed. Today the dragon is no longer the prerogative of the imperial court. It has become an image of the Chinese nation and a symbol of its civilization. Based on tradition, modern artists have created a new dragon culture, which transcends time with new artistic design. The new dragon relishes modern culture while preserving ancient tradition, and is an artistic representation of our time.

服饰 Garments

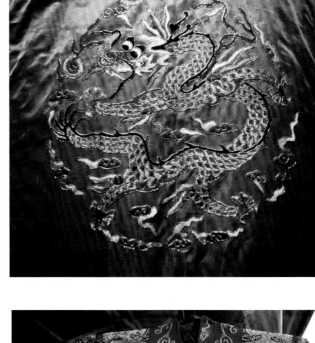

民间文物
Folk Collection

法华寺门前雕塑
Sculptures in front of Fahuasi Temple

现代工艺雕塑品
Modern Artifacts and Sculptures

皮影团龙造型
Coiling dragon figure in shadow-puppet play

剪纸
Paper-cut

中国年画
Chinese New Year Picture

各种材质现代工艺品
Modern Artefacts Made of
Various Materials

现代石雕工艺品
Modern Stone Sculptures

孔庙编钟
Ancient Chinese chime in the Confucius Temple

邮票
Stamps

2012 年发行的龙金币
Gold Coin Stamped with a Dragon

龙 摄影作品
Photos of Dragon

左上图为 砖雕拐子龙.
Upper left, dragon figure on brick carving

右上图为团龙图案的砖雕戗檐板。
Upper right, coiling dragons on brick carvings

龙的造型风筝
Kite of dragon design

帽挂
Hat stand

中国龙的造型大茶壶
Dragon shaped spout on tea pot

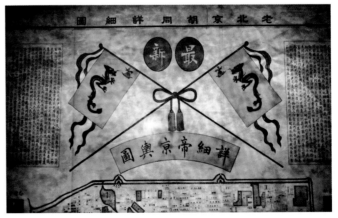

龙旗
Dragon flag

北京饭店喷泉
Fountain in front of Beijing Hotel

仿圆明园丢失喷泉龙头
Dragon figured nozzle, imitatation of one lost from the
Old Summer Palace

王府井遗址井盖
Cover of an ancient well in the Wafujing area of Beijing

龙造型工艺品
Artifacts with dragon design

宝剑 Swords

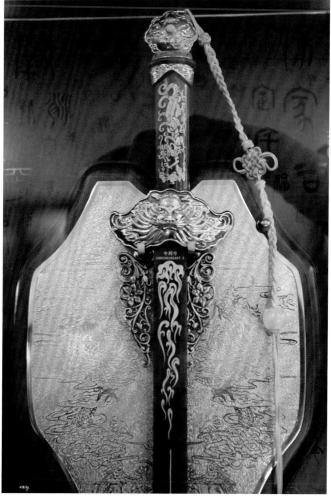

宝剑 Swords

相传龙的七子叫睚眦，好刑杀，常被装饰于刀柄剑鞘上。

Yazi, dragon's seventh child. Often chosen to be the decoration on the sheath of a sword due to its ferocious nature.

龙图案的现代陶瓷器具，韵味十足。

Charming dragon figures on modern porcelain.

各种龙图案的现代仿古玉石雕刻工艺品。
Various dragon figures on modern jade carvings in imitation of the ancient style.

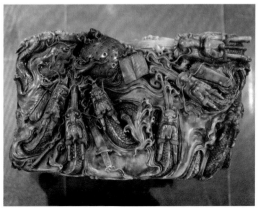

中央电视塔摄影作品
Photo montage: Dragon on China's Central TV Tower

香山碧云寺大门
The gate of Biyunsi Temple in Xiangshan Park

图书在版编目（CIP）数据

京华龙影 / 朱天纯著 . —北京 ：学苑出版社，
2012.4

ISBN 978-7-5077-3999-2

Ⅰ．①京… Ⅱ．①朱… Ⅲ．①龙－文化－北京市－摄
影集 Ⅳ．①B933-64

中国版本图书馆CIP数据核字（2012）第069776号

责任编辑：张　翔
英文翻译：王翔永
英文审稿：[英] Michael Crook
美术设计：徐道会
出版发行：学苑出版社
地　　址：北京市丰台区南方庄 2 号院 1 号楼
电　　话：010-67675512　67678944　67601101（邮购）
邮　　编：100079
网　　址：www.book001.com
电子邮箱：xueyuan@public.bta.net.cn
经　　销：新华书店
印　　刷：北京信彩瑞禾印刷厂
开　　本：889×1194　1/16
字　　数：10千字
印　　张：12.25
版　　次：2012年5月第1版
印　　次：2012年5月第1次印刷
印　　数：3000册
定　　价：120.00元